Once upon a time, there were three little pigs.

One day, they had a discussion and decided to build new houses for themselves.

The first little pig found lots of wheat and rice straw and decided to build a simple house with it.

He made the walls with wheat straw and the roof with rice straw.

He soon finished his new house and was very proud of it.

The second little pig had a different idea. He was going to build himself a beautiful house of wood.

He started work straight away, sawing planks and nailing them together.

After a very busy day he finally finished his wooden house, and was very proud of it.

But the third little pig wasn't in a hurry. He was still moving bricks with a little cart when his two brothers had finished their new houses.

He didn't want a house made of straw or wood. He wanted a strong brick house instead.

It took him a few days to build the brick house. The other two little pigs said, "Why do you need such a strong house anyway?"

In the forest there was an old wolf, and he had always wanted to eat the three little pigs.

The old wolf knocked on the door of the straw house and said, "Little Pig, let me in." "You're the old wolf! I will not open the door!" shouted the first little pig.

"Then I'll huff and I'll puff and I'll blow your house down," the old wolf said. So he huffed and he puffed and, sure enough, the straw house fell down.

The first little pig escaped just in time and ran away to hide in the second little pig's wooden house.

Next the wolf went to the wooden house and shouted, "Little Pig, let me in." "You're the old wolf! We will not let you in!" said the two little pigs.

"Then I'll knock your house down," the old wolf said and he threw himself at the wooden house. CRASH! Down went the wooden house!

The two little pigs sprang to their feet and ran into the third little pig's brick house. What a narrow escape!

The old wolf followed them and tried to knock down the brick house.

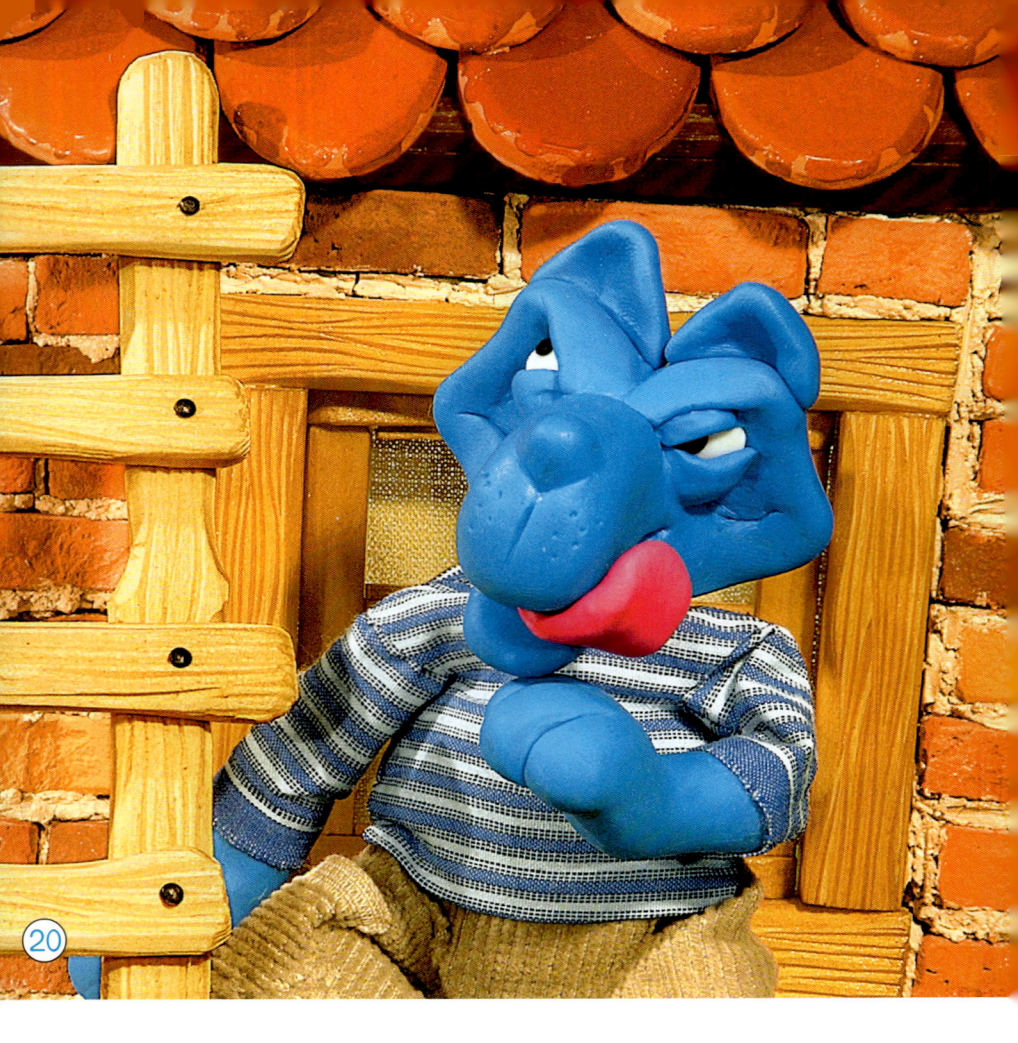

But the brick house was so strong that he could do it no harm at all. Then he had an idea.

Seeing a chimney on the roof, the old wolf fetched a ladder, rested it against the house and started climbing up.

The third little pig heard noises on the roof and said, "Let's make a big fire in the fireplace. Then the old wolf won't be able to get in."

As soon as the old wolf climbed into the chimney, his bottom caught fire, and he yelled out in pain.

The three little pigs said, "This brick house is amazing. We don't need to worry about the old wolf any more."